Rough Grace

Rough Grace

poems

Raphael Helena Kosek

Concrete Wolf
Poetry Chapbook Series

ISBN 978-0-9964754-0-2

Design: Tonya Namura using Gentium Book Basic

Cover art: Reproduced with the permission of Dorset Fine
Arts or © Dorset Fine Arts
Taqaiqsiqtu Tuttu (Resting Caribou) 2010
Kananginak Pootoogook
Stonecut and stencil, 56 cm x 34.7 cm
printed by Cee Pootoogook

Author photo: Kateri Kosek

Concrete Wolf Poetry Chapbook Series

Concrete Wolf
PO Box 1808
Kingston, WA 98346

http://ConcreteWolf.com
ConcreteWolf@yahoo.com

Acknowledgments

Some of the poems in this chapbook, or versions of them, have appeared in the following journals or magazines which the author gratefully acknowledges. Italicized poems are painting titles.

Catamaran: "*Pelvis with Moon*"

Coal Hill Review: "*Caribou Resting*"

Commonweal: "*The Miracle Flower*"

Holly Rose Review: "Holding Terror"

Lumina: "*Dark Iris No. 3,*" "The River"

Poetry East: "The Ship of You"

The Recorder: "*Sunflower, New Mexico*"

Silk Road: "Landscape sans Christina"

Sojourners: "What Van Gogh Saw"

Southern Humanities Review: "Always the River"

Contents

Rough Grace

"We have art in order not to die of the truth."
Friedrich Nietzsche

"Wherever art appears, life disappears."
Robert Motherwell

Caribou Resting 2010
Inuit stone cut and stencil, Kananginak Pootoogook

The two caribou ground me
frozen in their stone-cut repose
brown and white on sea-grey background
one floating above the other, perspective
be damned.

Legs folded neatly underneath
elegant bodies of speckled brown;
one looks behind, another
to the east. I imagine the sun
rising before their unblinking
eyes, the tundra awash in early light.

I want to read them like a book
of hours, to clear the unholy noise
that seizes me with its stuttering
traffic of dark and busy words.
I want the clarity of cold, the still
warm indentation their bodies must leave
in the snow, the musky animal scent
that means a different life
than this one. Let them
unfold their legs carefully

and raise the warm breathing
torsos up, rump first; the sickled legs
unbending, all grace as they wend
away, swift and soft like currents
of snowed air. And let me

feel the clear mind of the one
whose steady hand
    could balance them
        just so
on my calendar of days.

Pilgrims

A dog barks in solitary
obligation to the night

Shifting in their stalls
cattle exhale sweet breath

Hills slip into morning
rising out of mists that linger
reluctant for day's clarity

The sun's light is deflected, still,
to a feather pale moon
that dissipates into milk sky

and earth heaves into morning,
afternoon, evening,

following the slap of tides,
the lunge of beast to its burden

and yearnings of men
who can recall no other home
yet feel forever strange and amazed
here

as if they'd just stepped
off a ship from some far place
into the pitch and pith of this earth:

its birdsong—delirious,
its losses—stunning.

The River

I am not inclined to write of places.
A river, say, for if you don't know it
you will right away be bored,
tired to hear of some strange water,
how it flows and where it glitters.
Not interested to learn how the trees bend
over the river at such and such a spot
or how deer drink there, tentative,
in early amber light.

If I begin to tell you how
she loved and lost, you will say
I've heard that one before. How
she is crippled and mends herself
at the place where the trees bend
over the river in just such a way.
She has seen the deer, watched
their mincing progress, loved them
for their fear.

I could send a train along the river,
but then I'd have to tell you
what kind and how many cars.
And even I wouldn't care, but she might
hear its whistle and take it as an omen.

I could write about myself, how my pen
flickers over paper making green pictures.
But, by God, you've had enough
of Emily Dickinson with thousands of poems
under the bed, her hair pinned tightly,

the pale round face
peering into your soul.

So it's best, I think,
if you see this river for yourself.
The woman might be there sitting
on a stone, expecting the deer.
Or you might find yourself waving
from a green boat
heading north in amber light.

The Ship of You

All is foregone, the way light breaks
like tea infusing the morning sky,

the rounding swell of the horizon
cresting, the underside of the hawk's

wing where it traffics with the air.
So much is bought and sold. My finding

you is a bargain I don't know how
I managed, deserved—I

who always paid cold coin, and dearly,
for the things of this world. Now, I barter

my words for a streak of sunshine,
the chill night air, that cloud I called

luminous. A rum deal: it faded and all
but disappeared. Look, I am counting

your fingers, blessing your garments
and the haze of your hair, without price.

My mouth is round and full of rapture:
the fragrance of grapes in sun's heat,

buzzing of insects deep in the grasses,
a fey breeze that ripples the leaves.

I am lazy in my wealth of you, not eager
to spend it. You are the best book

I've ever opened, and if I never reach
the last page, my fortune will be untold.

I spy your enemies, mine, skirting the shore,
gauging the distance, marking us with

rumor of conflict, dangerous currents.
My cache of weapons on board will hold

them off with mesmerizing metaphor—words
like warriors, like gods—the ballast of this ship.

Dark Iris No. 3, 1927
Georgia O'Keeffe

Form rises out of fog,
two bodies lean into each other,
one nudging the other with gentled
wing, shifting shoulder, light heft
of hip—always there,
wavering as they come
and go in the quiet, keening grey
of petaled love.

Breathe, they say,
this is the dark and the light,
how they mingle. The dark
is no threat, it softens hard edges
like the marsh tide arriving

unnoticed, night blue petals
lapping at our feet—
the iris rising and falling like a lung,
fluent gills of a fish,
irrepressible sail.

Always the River: A Novel (abridged)

. . . and they paddled for days, the water
glinting hard in their eyes. Grey
is what happens to blue at twilight.

I know this is how the soul travels,
how we keep moving up river
from wherever we are—skimming past

trees in full frock, slippery banks, the blind
eyes of houses. *He says something to her
and she says something back.* Words like stones

tumbled and cool, precise or incidental. Movement
is what we have, water-spray—its blessing.
Around the next bend—catbird whistling

while moonlight's cold white money fills
our coffers. We pull the pale silver in earnest
ritual—through deceit, lust, forgiveness, the world's

wild holler—believing this is the way
as we cut the deep green dark, hungering like the
early explorers, hatless, brazen, from glory to glory.

Black and Purple Petunias, 1927

Georgia O'Keeffe

No richer black than purpled black:
languorous petals droop
on two velvet-swagged heads
of eggplant hue, two monkeys,
two lovers, two sad siblings bear
the tyranny of days and nights.

Do you see how hard it is for us,
how we hurdle through the trees,
leap through the hours,
tedious, bewildered?
But like siblings, one will be devious,
tease the other to tantrum.

Or lovers: one is insincere
and the other feels it in her embrace
but chooses to say nothing,
to be a good monkey
in this heavy, purple passage
where we find ourselves together.

Henri Rousseau Answers Questions

Because the white lake of canvas waits for me.
The lovely free space invites me to wander,
to arrive at some unforeseen destination.

No, I was never afraid of the distance
where France vanishes.
Did I say how grateful I am?
                                    Believe me,
I know all about Hamlet's nutshell—here,
I am king of a thousand leaves, animal eyes,
the bewildering body,

and my garden blooms without withering
and my garden overruns its borders
and my garden swells to the sea

where I skim the tender
curve of this blue world in the bright
boat I have fashioned. Look

at what falls into shadow, into
a hundred shades of green,
the splay of leaf and blossom

where person and panther connive,
where the tiger holds a deer-like creature
in its teeth, stilled in a frozen paradise.

You say I've made the savage and the exotic
curiously tame? Yes, the ripping of flesh is silent here
and the lion could almost lie down with the lamb.

Tiger in a Tropical Storm (Surprised) 1891
Henri Rousseau

The tropical winds bend the leaves,
bow the branches –
      and the tiger among them
hunches into a defensive crouch,
      teeth bared, ears back.
The invisible rain
      pelts the tiger
and his domain. An enemy
he cannot attack, it surrounds him
      like an army.

He is surprised like the man
who realizes
      halfway through his life
that he is constantly
      defending himself
against an unknown force that has
      no shape, no name,
yet leaves him breathless,
beaten, forever valiant.

Is the tiger diminished? Is the man?
The tiger's stripes and stealth,
      its singeing breath,
the tawny grist of its soul—
      Is it enough?
And the man? – who
      throws his sodden cape
      after the golden days

but watches each day trail off
        into a tangle of vine and shadow—
his words broken on the wind,
        scarlet leaves heavy
        drenched—and night
such bitter tea.

Bearing It

At twilight a man looks like a tree, a tree could be a man
in the soft charcoal. That mailbox looming up ahead
nearly moves like the young buck that crossed in front
of me yesterday, evaporating into the shadowy brush
where the houses end.

It could be my eyes.
It could be life.

The bare branch against the roseate blush of dusk
silhouettes a dove, plump and still, or a leaf
that autumn's frost did not drop, holding on
as I do to this life. Long have I marveled
that the sky could be an ocean—and remember
when you thought the clouds were mountains
and we laughed at your lovely error?

It could be your eyes.
It could be life.

I cannot tell if trouble is receding from me
like the tide, or like the tide will no doubt
find me again in six hours, six days, weeping
into a pillow, rising from the bitter wash.

Stars glitter; planets do not, but both are high and deep
and have parts in the opera of the night
where rest will come to me, bowed down, lowly—
and comfort—allotted by hands invisible.

Sunflower, New Mexico, II, 1935
Georgia O'Keeffe

You stand up fearless
in a sky so avid blue.

You think we don't have the simple heart
to rise up, knock our heavy heads

against Heaven, eat the sun
until our hair flames golden,

to kiss and wave in a never ending July.
Some of us do, but the weight

of all this wonder grows like a stone
and the sharp lace of early frost

sprouts a fine, low withering
that is not without its own eloquence.

Doing Laundry

Long-sleeve tee shirts,
        turquoise, heather grey,
blue steel—always one sleeve
        inside out.
Sweat pants: navy, charcoal,
        both legs never
        in sync: one leg
right way, the other, balled up,
        twisted. Always, I must
untangle the cotton-polyester limbs
        they pull off
of my father in the nursing home,
pockets tearing, seams
                giving way.

I have sewn them, fixed
        what is torn, ripped, wrinkled,
all the while grappling with
        the limbs of my father's
body: disobedient, rebellious,
so terribly ordinary, clumsy,
                beloved.
They laugh and joke
with "Mr. B." but the laundry
water is cold rinsing, reminding me
        of the flesh incarnate
inside these garments that dress
        mortality. The water

washes away only the strange
      white flecks, lotion
with a healthy reek, stains
      of uncontrollable living.
The second rinse cannot mask
      the cold that comes to visit
to sit with him every day,
and cannot be washed away.

Art and Life

from a painting of a working farm, Sheffield, MA by
Margaret Buchte

Why can't life be a painting I love—
the cows at the feed bin, "Room for One More"
says the title, the gentle hump of the Berkshires
behind them where the field runs soft
and blurry into aqua sky with a sun-blood red
cloud leaching into the cooler shades of evening
and a bald-faced cow gazing out at me.

And not the terror of these days—
the nursing home with all its inevitabilities,
the brusque efficiencies that surround
the dying, the point counterpoint
of aid and denial. My father, reduced
to eating, sleeping, excreting, maintains

the dignity and holiness of the ordinary,
the way saints must have looked
as the world ground them in its maw.
We could walk through these fields,
he and I, and there wouldn't need
to be conversation—just the cows,

and the crickets' low chirring
with fall easing in after summer,
the sweet scent of hay past perfect,
damp daze of the field, expectancy
of evening, the unseen life of night to come.

Barn with Snow, 1933
Georgia O'Keeffe

This barn fills the field of the canvas
with its warm heart, coolly covered
in a pristine blanket of snow, its windows
blank and grey, but we know, don't we,

the steaming breath of cows, their bovine
waft, gives life, gives home, gives purpose
no matter what has hooked us, pierced
our fragile bodies, troubled us in love,

orphaned us in the winter fields,
the rumbling mountains. If you cry,
the stolid walls will bolster you with
the strength of sweet lines, cloudy windows,

a living architecture proclaiming the world
is right because though cold and dark and clean
on the outside, the mess of life sings sweetly within
of shit and milk and hay—such rough grace.

What Van Gogh Saw

Van Gogh saw
the way our hearts burn
like the pinwheel stars
swirling in the night-mad sky,

the way our spirits,
bent and bruised in life's field,
reach endlessly upward
like the cypress trees
  full of knotty whorls
curling upwards
  to mingle with
and plead benediction
  from the sea-waved sky,

the way wild-maned sunflowers
are almost dizzy with themselves
and the power of heavy seed
flaming within them.

Lose an ear
lose your mind
lose your life

while crows scatter
  over the wheat field
and Lazarus forever rises
  under a fiery sun.

Common Mercies

"So little do we prize common mercies when we have
them to the full."

from *The Narrative of the Captivity and Restoration of
Mrs. Mary Rowlandson,* 1676

You should be so grateful
for the smooth sheets,
        quiet slide
into sleep, haloed tree
outside your window.
        Grateful
for the dull day where
no glass shatters, no voice
is raised, where you can
        wander room to room,
let the unimportant minutes tick by
        unnoticed. Grateful
for the bread, full and soft
        in your mouth,
for your children—
        smarter, quicker, better
than you—ringing
        like the sure bell
we are all supposed to be.

Because you *know*
what can happen:
        Fire blooms,
        the curtain, torn,
        the face, hardened.
A red man at the window.

As My Daughter Plays the Piano

Brahms finds the bright heart of the day
        and darkens it,
plunging down to black waters,
        restlessly seeking
consolation, roaming the notes in
        gusting quest so unconsoled.

Her fingers flicker over the keys,
animate the peacocks
        in the wallpaper,
set adrift its brimming roses,
        until each note gleams
and wavers in the household air

now singing desolation,
                now triumph,
weary of returning to itself—
        A word, a note, a person—
how tireless we are supposed to be

        beginning over and over,
indefinite as the A minor Intermezzo
        wandering toward gorgeous
uncertain resolution

        in little flaming suicides
ever threatening that abrupt
        and easeful quiver,
the ebony stilled and silent.

Holding Terror

down. I am always just
　　　holding terror
down. What if she . . . What if
he . . . doesn't mean what
she . . . What if two, or more,
　　　collide?
　　　If the surgeon
slips, or the last step
gives way. . . if the child
wandering the woods has
　　　no bread crumbs
　　　　　　nothing
like it? What if
　　　I cannot bear
morning's fingers
　　　prying open the day
or night's full moon
whitewashing my bedroom
　　　white pages
turning, turning into
the winking, yawning
round earth disengaging
　　　from the universe
spinning away into falling
　　　like falling in dreams
where we never feel
　　　the bottom (waking
first) but now I shall know
that jettison, the way truth
　　　bends metal, riddles
　　　the windshield

while the wheel
        comes off
in my hands, roadless
        the sea
rolling in
        restless, grey.

Seascape

When I close my eyes in cover of trees
at the edge of salt marsh, wind
      moving through oak and pine
          sounds like rain.
How curious that wind could be water,
      one thing, another.

The smell of salt, mud flats
      when the tide goes out
recalls the body, when honest sweat
      assures us of the good animal
within, our days measured against
      the fluid drift of clouds.
Yet we cleave to our identities,
wearing them like clothes, lipsticked in,
      cinched with a belt.

      Don't you feel
the way wind runs through us, water
always pulls us,
      how bird song trills
from our throats,
      how we disappear
with the last light, waver
      with the first star?

Lunch with Still Life Flowers and My Mother

Brick walls,
    hearty ballast of this luncheon,
bedecked with some enterprising painter's
    exuberant poppies, waving tulips,
 we lean long into our booth,
    lunch already such a common place
on Tuesdays, Thursdays, we know the menu
    by heart . . . so we are happy
when they change the paintings.
Me, partial to landscapes . . . but these flowers
    are portraits in oil, each one a lesson
    in how to be still,
    to bloom from within.
A green-tinged iris, demure calla lily,
sunflowers' riotous gold on a background
of purples and blues; modern, intense, "Wild
    with energy" says my mother
who always loved art and sees
    with the artist's eye at eighty-three
when her body is no longer
    who she used to be, when some
unknown invader broods
    under her flesh.

Appointments await us like Cerberus
    at the gate. Pray for a simple death.
Daughter-mother, mother-daughter.
Nothing is easy is what I know,
    so let's have lunch:
    Coffee? Yes, I'll have some more.
Dessert today, ladies? No, thank you.

We are full. We are heavy
like the flowers that bend and flare
     on the rustic brick walls.

We are done with time, we dine,
     we lunch, we leave the dear
young waitress a good tip
     as if it paves the road to heaven,
and she will say a prayer for my mother;
     we accept them likes coins,
shiny, significant, compiling grace
     unto grace.

Landscape sans Christina

upon reading an old interview with Andrew Wyeth
just after his death

"Lonely" my mother complains
about the paintings hanging
on my walls bereft of people:
       late winter sun
bruising the silent snow, but no
stark figure bundled against the cold.
       A river toils out to sea
where no one paddles a modest boat
or stands on the bridge to fish—only
the grass in collusion with the wind
where a dusty-eyed child might be
       dreaming summer away
but isn't. Then I wonder

could there even be
       a paradise
without Adam and Eve—
       their restless hunger, desirous
       eye, fingers entwined
in the wild green hair
       of plants, the friction
       of flesh, their trembling
when a tree falls?

Andrew Wyeth sometimes regretted
painting Christina
       into "Christina's World,"
believing that
       from the weathered grey

of the sentinel house,
       the gunmetal gleam
of the ocean always
       just over the rise,
field inclining upwards to meet
       the paled sky,
we should *feel* her presence
yearning in that sea of grass
endlessly grounded, her lovely
       and crippled
body, redundant, after all.

When

When my father was dying
I was so asleep and so awake, that night
was as nothing to me as I crawled out
        into morning, another visit
to the home where wheelchairs
made me dizzy with their rolling,
even when they were parked and still,
like chariots blazing into another world
        invisible to me.

When the warmth of an Indian summer day
called me to take my father down
on the elevator and outside to feel
        the real sun on his skin,
(not what the windows which do not open allow),
time curdled in his cup, stilled
        in the long, lazy sun.

When I walk into his room,
find him dozing, he wakes quickly
with, "How nice—glad to see you!"
and something curls around my heart
        with such strange fingering -
offered up to the mountain
        outside his window
where the trees bristle before winter,
when we bare ourselves
        to a sky, vast and irretrievable.

Pelvis with Moon, 1943
Georgia O'Keeffe

White angel, balustrade of bone,
the bluest piece of sky
is framed in your elegant portal
as you buttress the bone moon
on your bleached hip

where warm flesh, haunch of steer
or pony, procreational pivot
once saddled you to your spent mortality
where you breathed red dust
roamed blue mountains

where your stony eye rolled white
and wild when the man encircled you
with his rope. Such pink living,
such beaten paths so far
from the sea

and now your gleaming bone
resembles nothing so much
as a pierced and dazzling whorl
of shell with the sea of sky
leaking through, a windy
trumpet of soundless music,
a gorgeous vacancy
unbridled, no longer ridden
or driven or dreaming,
but a window to heavenly space.

The Miracle Flower, 1936
Georgia O'Keeffe

Our white bells
trumpet the miracle
of large, open whiteness.

Don't you see how
we fill this world,
her tired canvas,
with buoyant promise?

We are the mind unjumbled,
excellent voice that calls
the dark spin of your life
into question. Our opening

shuts the door on doubt,
our lifting heads wag in blue wind,
gracious leaves curl in concert
with the white stretch of our throats.

We are never far from ourselves
like you,
yet we lean into blue sky
and that is miracle enough.

About the Author

Raphael Kosek was born and lives in New York's beautiful Hudson Valley where she graduated Vassar College with departmental honors in English and a distinguished thesis of her own poetry. She has an MA in American literature from Western Connecticut State University and she currently teaches American literature and creative writing at Marist College and SUNY Dutchess Community College in Poughkeepsie, New York.

When she began writing poetry at age twelve, it never seemed a choice, just something she had to do; but after college, teaching high school and raising children pulled her away until she returned to poetry with renewed dedication in midlife after a long hiatus. A heightened love of art also has taken hold of her and she cannot get enough of paintings, finding that the creative spark of image and color jumps like fire to the page igniting response in poems. She believes that when she writes a poem, she never knows where she's going, but that she wants to go there, must go there.

Her first chapbook, *Letting Go*, 2009, was published by Finishing Line Press in their New Women's Voices series. Her poetry has appeared in *The Chattahoochee Review*, *Catamaran*, *Big Muddy*, *Still Point Arts Quarterly*, and *Water-Stone*. She has been the recipient of two Arts Mid-Hudson fellowships for her poetry and a first prize winner in the international contest of *Deus Loci*.

www.ingramcontent.com/pod-product-compliance
Lightning Source LLC
Chambersburg PA
CBHW032104040426
42449CB00007B/1184